Life in the Spirit Seminar for Children

Adapted from the Life in the Spirit Seminar
by Jerry Munk

TABOR HOUSE
www.taborpub.com

Cover design by James Munk

Table of Contents

Introduction

The whole of the Christian life can be summed up in one word: grace. Grace is God's undeserved gifts, which He pours into our life each and every day. Through God's grace I came to know Jesus Christ as my Lord and Savior. Through His grace I was baptized in the Holy Spirit. Through His grace I was introduced to the Work of Christ Community, where I received the teaching, fellowship, and tangible support needed to sustain my Christian life through the years. And, through His grace I met and married a wonderful Christian woman: my wife Jan.

The Lord has continued to pour His grace into our family. When our children were quite young, many parents in our community came to the conclusion that our children should share fully in our life together—including the charismatic aspect of that life. We began praying for them to be baptized in the Holy Spirit, and they were. About this time, the community developed a special prayer meeting so the children could experience charismatic worship with their peers. We also made room for the children to exercise their charismatic gifts in the adult gatherings. In addition, the Work of Christ began a summer children's camp. The week contained all of the things you would expect: games, crafts, boats, swimming, and, of course, camp food. It also featured a lot of activities aimed at spiritual development. But, the most important event at camp was the "Gathering for Christ" where we would pray for the children to be baptized in the Holy Spirit. At camp, the children would be prayed with year after year: not because what happened the previous year did not "stick" but because the children had matured and were ready for more.

The charismatic life is not just about summer camp and prayer meetings; it is mostly about day-to-day life. Families in our community were encouraged to have family prayer—including charismatic prayer—on a regular basis. This, too, was a gift of God's grace.

Somewhere in all of this, it seemed right to take our own children, one by one, through the Life in the Spirit Seminar. We wanted to be personally involved in our children's spiritual life and to share with them this material that had been so pivotal in our own lives. For several weeks in a row, Jan and I would sit down with one of our children and work through the outlines with them—making the content understandable at a child's level. (I have a strong opinion that it is especially helpful for Dad to be the visible leader in all of this, but I will spare you that lecture.) When it was time for the prayer session, we invited another family for the Lord's Day meal and afterwards prayed with the child to be baptized in the Holy Spirit.

What a blessing it has been to see our children grow up living a Spirit-filled Christian life. They were blessed with regular opportunities to exercise their spiritual gifts at both children and adult gatherings. They first attended and then served at summer camp. They participated in regional youth retreats and conferences. They went on mission trips, joined University Christian Outreach, and lived in Christian household. As young adults, they, and many of their peers in the community, have a maturity in the Holy Spirit that comes from many years of living in the Holy Spirit.

This book is my attempt to share this blessing with your family. *"You will receive the gift of the Holy Spirit. This promise is for you. It is also for your children"* (Acts 2:38&39 ICB).

How to Use this Book

This is a book to read out loud to your children, but you should read it differently than you would a story book—say *The Lord of the Rings* by JRR Tolkein. The difference is that *The Lord of the Rings* is Tolkein's story. You start at the beginning, and, to get the whole story, you read straight through to the end. This book, however, is not just my story, it is not just my experience; it is your story and your experience too. Soon, it is to be hoped, it will be your child's experience. As such, you should not just start at the beginning and read to the end. Instead, read a little and then stop and talk for a bit. If everything works well, you might discover that you spend more time talking than reading.

What should you talk about?

First, you should talk about your experience. You will read, for example, the section on making a personal commitment to Jesus Christ. That is something you have done, and here is a wonderful opportunity to tell that part of your story to your child: how you came to this decision in your life, what changed as a result of that decision, and how that

3

decision has formed your life over the years. In another section you will read about being baptized in the Holy Spirit. Again, that is something that happened to you. Your child will be interested in how it happened, what you experienced, and how your Christian life is different because of that event.

Talking with your child about your experiences is not just sharing the history of your life with them—although that is good too. It helps them to see that the Lord can and does work in the lives of real people: people they know well. Seeing this helps children have faith that God will work in their lives too. It also will give them a sense of how the Lord works in people's lives—how an individual can engage the grace of God and grow into Christian maturity over time.

Second, you should talk about your church. This book is written for an ecumenical audience. As such, it says some very general things about topics on which your church tradition has some very specific teaching. The book, for example, mentions baptism. Your church, to be sure, has a worked-out position on baptism: what happens, when it should happen, how it should happen, and how baptism relates to your child at this point in his or her life. You will want to give you child some supplemental explanation that fills out their understanding from the point of view of your family's church tradition.

Finally, talk about questions. The material in this book, I sincerely hope, will lead to questions. If your child asks a question, stop, and take the time necessary to answer it well. If your child does not ask a question, you might want to ask it instead: "So, Susie, can you remember what is God's plan for your life? What do you think that means for you?" Asking questions helps you determine if your child really understands the material, helps teach the material, and helps you make a pastoral judgment: is my child personally appropriating the material?

Is My Child Ready?

This is an important question, and the answer comes in two parts: is my child ready cognitively, is my child ready spiritually.

The cognitive question centers on the child's ability to understand and apply the material. Some children will be able to understand and apply these concepts as young as nine. Others may need to wait until age 12. Determining factors include obvious things like the child's intelligence, maturity, level of interest, but also less obvious factors like his or her ability to sit still and pay attention. I think it is helpful if the child is able to read at some level. The reason for this is that being baptized in the Holy Spirit typically makes the Bible come "alive" in the life of the individual. If the child is able to read, this important aspect of the charismatic life can develop in his or her life.

Spiritual readiness centers on the child's relationship with the Lord: have they made an (age-appropriate) commitment of their life to Jesus Christ: do they understand what this means, have they made an actual decision for Christ (or personally affirmed their baptismal vows), and are they living that decision in a responsible (for a child) way? A parental/pastoral judgment is required.

Some children will be doing well with their Christian commitment. Some, however, may not be doing that well. The first two chapters of this book are evangelistic in nature: they lay out the basic Gospel message and encourage a personal response to Jesus Christ. If your child has not yet come into a living, personal relationship with Jesus Christ, you can go through the first two chapters with him or her and help them make that important connection. If they make it, that is great—keep going through the Seminar. If they are not ready to make a personal commitment to Jesus (they do not understand the concept, they do not want to follow Jesus, or whatever) it would not be appropriate to keep moving ahead with the Seminar. In some cases the solution is just to wait a while. Come back to the evangelistic presentation in six months. Not only will the child be six months older, your initial presentation of the Gospel will have had time to "perk" in their heart and mind. In other cases, maturity is not so much a factor but some kind of rebellion against God. The dynamics of this situation exceeds the limits of this little book. Please talk to your pastor at church, your community pastoral worker, or your small group to help develop a plan.

The Prayer Session

The prayer session (Chapter 5) is the apex of the seminar. Make it a significant event in the life of your child. There is a note to Mom and Dad just before that section, please read it well in advance so you can make appropriate preparation.

After the Prayer Session

Those of us who have been baptized in the Holy Spirit for some time know that it is not the end of the journey but a step (a big step) along the journey. Chapters 6 & 7 begin to build upon the seminar by encouraging a life filled with prayer, scripture, service, and Christian community. Do take a pastoral concern for your children: help them to appropriate these elements of the Christian life.

Should we pray with children to be baptized in the Holy Spirit?

Baptized in the Spirit—What Do We Mean?

This is a difficult question made even more complicated by the fact that the Sword of the Spirit is an ecumenical community of communities, and different church traditions vary in understandings and practices.

It might be best to start by saying what I do not mean by the term "baptized in the Holy Spirit."

I am not saying that the Holy Spirit is not present or at work in an individual before they are prayed with to be baptized in the Spirit. The Holy Spirit is present and at work in every believer—even those not yet confirmed or chrismated. ("Chrismation" is the term used in the Christian East—both Orthodox and Eastern-Rite Catholic—for the "sacrament" or "mystery" that more or less corresponds to Confirmation in the West.) 1 Corinthians 12:3 says

"No one can say that Jesus Christ is Lord except by the Holy Spirit." If we take this verse at face value, the Holy Spirit brings people to the point of making Jesus the Lord of their life. Therefore the Holy Spirit is at work in some way early on. The Catechism of the Catholic Church makes this point well when it says that baptism "gives them the power to live and act under the prompting of the Holy Spirit through the gifts of the Holy Spirit" (#1266).

Furthermore I am not saying a person receives complete fullness and maturity in the ministry, gifts, and fruit of the Holy Spirit when prayed with for the baptism in the Holy Spirit. The Apostle Peter is a good example of this. In John 20:22, Jesus breathes on His disciples (including Peter) and says "receive the Holy Spirit." One can only assume that Peter received the Holy Spirit at that moment. In Acts 2, Peter is there when the Holy Spirit is poured out on the day of Pentecost. But just two chapters later Peter is again present as "they were all filled with the Holy Spirit" (Acts 4:31). Simeon the New Theologian says, "The purpose of the Christian life is to acquire the Holy Spirit." Growing in the Spirit is never accomplished, but is an ongoing process.

I am not equating baptism in the Holy Spirit with the sacrament of confirmation/chrismation or implying that the sacramental act is in any way deficient. Not all Christian traditions hold confirmation/chrismation as a sacrament, but those that do (to the very best of my knowledge) would not say that the Holy Spirit is absent from a Christian until the sacrament is administered, nor would they say that a Christian who receives the sacrament has experienced, at that point, everything the Holy Spirit wants to do in his or her life.

What is in a Name?

The term "baptized in the Holy Spirit" was, near as I can tell, an orphaned phrase up to the Pentecostal awakening at the turn of the 20th century (i.e., the phrase did not seem to be commonly used in older writings). It was adopted by the Pentecostals and later picked up by the Charismatic Renewal. Literally, the term means to be "immersed in the Holy Spirit." If you ask an informed Pentecostal Christian what the phrase means, you will get one answer: one that reflects Pentecostal theology and thinking. If you ask an informed Catholic charismatic what it means, you will get a decidedly different answer: one that reflects Catholic theology and thinking. This is not all that unusual: many Biblical and theological terms morph a bit as you move from one tradition to another.

Back when I was working in the Orthodox Charismatic Renewal, we avoided the term—mainly to avoid misunderstanding. Instead we used terms like "release of the Spirit" or "greater openness to the Spirit." While these phrases may be less controversial in some situations, they suffer from not being very "catchy" or Biblical. I am happy to use "baptized in the Spirit," and I am equally happy to explain what I mean by this phrase as an Orthodox charismatic Christian.

So, What Do We Mean?

When I pray with a Christian to be baptized in the Holy Spirit, I presume that person already has the Holy Spirit at work within them. I also assume that they are not <u>completely</u> experiencing the life, the work, the fruit, and the gifts of the Holy Spirit. (I am not experiencing the Holy Spirit <u>completely</u>, and neither are you.) This is not to say that I think everyone is at the same place: people can be at various places along a continuum. All I am saying is that no one in this life achieves perfection.

Sometimes, what I am praying for is a brand new openness to the Holy Spirit. A person may have been baptized, or baptized and confirmed or chrismated, but have little personal awareness or experience of the Holy Spirit in their life (a not-uncommon state of affairs). In this situation, my prayer would be, that the Holy Spirit (who is already in them) would be released (by them) to work in their life—that the individual will be open to the Holy Spirit's work and gifts in a new way. The charismatic experience of being baptized in the Spirit is one of coming into a personal relationship with the Holy Spirit (i.e. to experience the person of the Holy Spirit personally), to become open to the gifts of the Holy Spirit operating in one's life, and to begin worshipping the Lord in a particularly charismatic way: loud praise and worship with room given to exercise the gifts of the Spirit. This, at least, is how I am using the term in this book.

Sometimes, however, I pray with people who have already been "baptized in the Spirit" for an even greater release of and openness to the Holy Spirit. This kind of prayer does not imply that there is anything wrong with the Holy Spirit who is at work within them. The prayer is rather meant for a greater yielding and openness to the work, gifts, grace, and fruit of the Holy Spirit. This would be very much in the sense of Paul's instruction to Timothy: "Therefore I remind you to stir up the gift of God which is in you through the laying on of my hands" (2 Timothy 1:6).

In the case of children, however, we may be praying for a Christian who has not yet been confirmed/chrismated. In an ecumenical setting, it is difficult to say with certainty what adults believe the child has or has not yet received, because we believe different things about the sacrament—or even if this is a sacrament. Still, if a child is able to say that Jesus Christ is the Lord of their life, we know the Holy Spirit is present and active in them. This work may be confirmed and sealed at some later time, but the Holy Spirit is there and already at work.

That the less-than-fully initiated may receive the Holy Spirit can be seen in Acts 10:44 where the Holy Spirit falls upon the Gentile believers who later received baptism. The Catechism of the Catholic Church says that the Holy Spirit is received at baptism and from that point on initiates can experience the charismatic gifts: "The Most Holy Trinity gives the baptized sanctifying grace...giving them the power to live and act under the prompting of the Holy Spirit through the gifts of the Holy Spirit" (#1266).

To me, it seems perfectly reasonable to pray with a less-than-fully initiated Christian. We ask that the Holy Spirit would be released in his/her life in a fuller, richer way and that the individual would be open to whatever the Holy Spirit wants to do. What seems unreasonable to me is the idea of withholding this from a child who loves Jesus and has committed his or her life to Him. Again, the Catechism of the Catholic Church speaks to this point: "preparation for confirmation should aim at leading the Christian toward...a more lively familiarity with the Holy Spirit—his actions, his gifts, and his biddings" (#1309). [Of course for Christians in the Eastern Churches— both Orthodox and Catholic—our children are chris-

11

mated as infants, so the logic is a little different.] It seems to me, that being prayed with to be baptized in the Holy Spirit (for the release of the Holy Spirit, and/or for greater openness to the work of the Holy Spirit—you pick the phrase) is appropriate both before and after confirmation.

The Special Situation with Children

In my community, The Work of Christ, we pray with children to become more and more open to the work of the Holy Spirit in their life. Because children are gaining both ability and maturity year by year, we tend to pray with them with some regularity. One year we may pray that the Spirit will give them a gift of boldness; the next year, the gift of tongues; and the year after that, discernment. While some may say that the child receives "more of the Holy Spirit," I think it would be more accurate to say that the child becomes more and more yielded to the work of the Holy Spirit. Of course praying for people with some regularity should not be limited to children. Adults too, can be prayed with in the same way, but usually not as often because they are not changing as rapidly as the children.

Because our children have been prayed with for a charismatic outpouring of the Spirit (yet another term) they are able to participate fully in the worship of the community. Many of our children speak and sing in tongues, offer prophecy, and receive scripture passages for the body (less regularly at adult-oriented gatherings, more regularly at children-oriented gatherings). They also pray out loud and in a similar way as their charismatic parents. I think this is very good for the children, and it is very good for the community. It seems to me unreasonable to expect children to participate charismatically in a charismatic prayer meeting if they have not been baptized in the Holy Spirit. Therefore, if we want our children to engage in the life of the community fully, we should pray with them to be baptized in the Holy Spirit.

A Caution?

The main caution I have about our practice is, that parents and children might relate to being prayed over as a "mission accomplished." People, adults and children alike, actually need to walk in the Holy Spirit. It is important for children to have regular opportunities to worship God charismatically and to exercise the gifts of the Spirit. One reason for our children's gatherings is that it gives our children a prayer meeting where the adults are not going to "carry" them. They have to seek the Lord themselves and be open to his work.

Sometimes young people in high school and college will say: "I don't need to be prayed with to be open to the Holy Spirit—that happened back in 5th grade at summer camp." The question is not what happened in the past, it is what is happening in your life today!

Some Final Notes

Bible Translations

Because this book is aimed at children, I wanted to use Bible passages that are understandable to children. I have used several translations to accomplish this goal: the *New International Children's Bible ®*, the *Good News Bible, Today's English Version ®, The Revised Standard Version ®*, and the *New King James Version ®*. In addition, I have taken the liberty of writing a paraphrase of several passages. Feel free to keep a translation you trust handy. It never hurts to look up a passage in your own Bible—just to be sure.

The Sword of the Spirit

This book was written for members of the Sword of the Spirit, an international, ecumenical association of charismatic communities. As such, it makes reference to several elements of community life without much explanation. If you are not a member of the Sword of the Spirit some of this jargon may be a little confusing, but now you know from whence it comes.

My Debt to the LSS

I cannot take credit as the author of this book. I just adapted *The Life in the Spirit Seminar* to a younger audience. Steve Clark was the primary author of the original *Life in the Spirit Seminar* and I very much appreciate his work. I have attempted to follow the LSS outlines relatively closely. My goal is not to teach our children something different from what we all received through the LSS, just to cut the "meat" into child-sized pieces. When I succeed, the credit really belongs to the original author. When I fail, the fault is my own.

Dedication

The Work of Christ Summer Camp has been tremendously instrumental in bringing our three children into a vibrant relationship with the Lord. I am thankful to all of the wonderful brothers and sisters who graciously served Jesus Christ, our community, and our children at camp. Therefore, this book is dedicated to the Work of Christ Camp staff and especially to our camp directors over the past 35 years: Jim deSpelder, Paul Carr, Bob Ceru, John and Marcia DeWitt, and Jon and Lori Ludwig. You have been the hands and the face of Jesus Christ to our family.

Note to Moms and Dads: *There is a lot of material in this chapter. It's not necessary for your child to understand every concept at this point. This chapter is an overview. We will return to some of the themes presented here and discuss them in greater detail in future chapters. The two main goals for this chapter are to (1) present the basic plan of salvation and (2) to introduce the concept of being baptized in the Holy Spirit. Our pastoral attention should primarily be focused on this question: Does my child believe in God and is he or she committing his or her life to Jesus Christ. Those from a sacramental background may say, "My child has been baptized, of course he or she is a Christian." Parents need, however, to look a little deeper—is the child personally embracing his or her baptismal vows and freely giving his or her life to Jesus? If your child is not ready to take this step, it would be best to set aside this seminar and focus instead on the more pressing issue of their making a personal commitment to Jesus Christ.*

At the end of each chapter are several scripture passages for your child to read and think about in his/her daily prayer time. There are also two chapters from the Bible that your child can read—or you can read to them—outside of their daily prayer time. Establishing a pattern of prayer and Bible reading is an important dynamic of the Life in the Spirit Seminars. Your child may need your help (encouragement and advice) to pray every day.

Chapter 1

I am the way, the truth, and the life;
no one comes to the Father except through me.
John 14:6 (NKJV)

God's Plan for My Life

Did you know that God has a plan for your life?

God created you so that you can know Him, love Him, serve Him, and live with Him forever. That is His plan for you. It's a very good plan—everything that comes from God is good. God wants you to love Him, because He loves you. He loves you just the way you are. He loves you even when you do bad things. The Bible says: *True love is God's love for us, not our love for God* (1 John 4:10 ICB). Even though God loves you, He gives you a choice: you can accept God, His love and His plan for your life, or you can say no to Him. It really is your choice. You accept God's plan for you by allowing Jesus, God's Son, to become your Lord, your Savior, and your friend. Let's talk about God's plan.

Life in All Its Fullness

A long time ago, Jesus said: *I came to give life— life in all its fullness* (John 10:10 ICB). God wants the very best for us. He wants each of us to have a full and happy life. He wants us to know Him, enjoy His love, and love Him in return. He also wants His children (you and me and everyone else who loves Him) to have good relationships with each another.

This sounds like a really nice plan, but many people do not have this kind of life. What keeps people from having what God wants them to have?

Sin Keeps People from God's Plan

Everyone has heard of the word "sin" but not everybody knows what it means. To sin means to disobey God. If we do not do what God wants us to do, that is "sin."

Jesus said that He came to give us life, and the Bible warns us that sin brings just the opposite. *When someone sins, he earns what sin pays—death* (Romans 6:23 ICB). That is why sin is such a problem, because it keeps us from what God wants for us. Jesus Christ brings life but sin brings death.

Another verse in the Bible warns us how sin works against God's plan. *Because those people chose not to know God...they are filled with every kind of sin, evil, selfishness, and hatred* (Romans 1:28-29 P). God wants people to have a good, full, and happy life, but sin keeps us from having what God wants us to have.

What I have to say next may be hard to hear, but it's the truth. You and I have sinned too—we have disobeyed God. The Bible says, *everyone has sinned and is far away from God's saving presence* (Romans 3:23 TEV). It does not say that only some people have sinned, but that everyone has—you and me included. Another Bible verse says it even more clearly: *If we say that we have no sin, we are fooling ourselves* (1 John 1:8 ICB).

Jesus Christ is the Way to God

You might ask, "How do we get to have a relationship with God if we are separated from Him because of sin?" That is a good question, and here is the answer. God's only Son became a man: Jesus Christ. Jesus never sinned—not even once. Because Jesus never sinned, and because He is God, He has power over sin and death that you and I do not. Through His death and resurrection Jesus made a way for people to know God now and live with Him through all time. *God so loved the world that He sent His only Son; whoever believes in Him will not perish but have eternal life* (John 3:16 P).

Jesus Christ is the only one who can take away your sin and make you right with God. Through Him you can know God's love and share in God's life with others. Jesus said: *I am the way, the truth, and the life; no one comes to the Father except through me* (John 14: 6 NKJV). Your Mom and Dad can not make you right with God. You can not even do it yourself. No one can come to Father God unless they come through Jesus Christ, His Son. But what does it mean to come to the Father through Jesus?

You Must Accept Jesus as Your Lord and Savior

Accepting Jesus as your Lord and Savior is more than just believing that Jesus is God and that He died to save you—but it is important to believe this truth about Jesus. Accepting Jesus is more than being a good person and obeying the teaching of Jesus—but it is important to be good and to obey Him.

Accepting Jesus as your Lord means that you decide to give your life to Him. It means that Jesus is not just a little part of your life, or even a big part of it; it means that you allow Him to become the center of your life. In a very real way, you belong to Jesus: your life is no longer your own because now you belong to Jesus.

When we accept Jesus—when He becomes the Lord of our life—we become children of God. The Bible says: *To those who believed in Him, He gave the right to become children of God* (John 1:12 P). This verse is really exciting, not only is Jesus our Lord and Savior, we can become children of God, so Jesus also becomes our brother and God becomes our Father.

Some people are baptized as infants and their parents and godparents say that Jesus is the Lord of the baby's life. If you were baptized as an infant, you still have a decision to make. Now that you are growing up, are you going to continue to make Jesus the Lord of your life? Are you going to belong to Him and make Him the center of your life? It is an important decision.

Some people wait until they are older to be baptized. If you have not yet been baptized, you too have a decision to make. Are you going to make Jesus the Lord of your life? Are you going to belong to Him and make Him the center of your life? It is an important decision. If you decide to give your life to Jesus, you should talk to your parents about how you can be baptized.

Receiving the Holy Spirit

Living for Jesus is hard. Jesus knows that it is too hard for us to do all by ourselves, so He promised to send the help that we need. Jesus said: *I will ask the Father, and He will give you another helper. He will give you this helper to be with you forever. The helper is the Spirit of truth* (John 14:16-17 ICB). The Holy Spirit is God, just like the Father is God, and His Son Jesus is God. There is just one God, but there are three persons: the Father, the Son, and the Holy Spirit. We can't understand this truth about God completely, but it is something that Christians believe because this is what the Bible teaches.

The Holy Spirit gives us the power that we need to live for Jesus. Jesus said: *The Holy Spirit will come to you; then you will receive power* (Acts 1:8 ICB). The Holy Spirit also gives us special gifts to help us live for Jesus together: *The gifts of the Spirit are given to each one so that everyone is helped* (1 Corinthians 12:7 P). And, the Holy Spirit helps us to act more like Jesus: *The Spirit gives love, joy, peace, patience, kindness, goodness, faithfulness, gentleness, and self-control* (Galatians 5:22 ICB).

This little book is about receiving the power of the Holy Spirit in a new way. If you are a Christian, the Holy Spirit is already at work in your life, but He wants you to experience Him in new and powerful ways. We call this being baptized in the Spirit.

To help you get ready to ask the Holy Spirit to work in this new way, let's read some stories from the Bible about what happened when people were baptized in the Holy Spirit.

When the day of Pentecost came, they (the apostles and some others) were all together in one place. Suddenly a noise came from heaven. It sounded like a strong wind blowing. This noise filled the whole house where they were sitting. They saw something that looked like flames of fire. The flames were separated and stood over each person there. They were all filled with the Holy Spirit and they began to speak in tongues [languages they did not know]. The Holy Spirit was giving them the power to speak these languages (Acts 2:1-4 ICB).

When Peter and John arrived, they prayed that the Samaritan believers might receive the Holy Spirit. These people had been baptized in the name of the Lord Jesus, but the Holy Spirit had not entered any of them. Then, when the two apostles began laying their hands on the people, they received the Holy Spirit (Acts 8: 15-17 ICB).

[Peter is making a speech.] "Everyone who believes in Jesus will be forgiven. God will forgive his sins through Jesus. All the prophets say this is true." While Peter was still saying this, the Holy Spirit came down on all those who were listening. The Jewish believers, who came with Peter, were amazed that the gift of the Holy Spirit had been given even to non-Jewish people. Because they heard them speaking in tongues [languages they did not know] and praising God. Then Peter said, "Can anyone keep these people from being baptized with water? They have received the Holy Spirit just as we did!" (Acts 10:43-48 ICB)

Chapter 1
Bible Readings

Over the next week, please read John 1 and Colossians 1. The book of John is one of the four Gospels: books that tell the story of Jesus Christ. The first chapter of John tells us about Jesus Christ and the very beginning of His ministry. Colossians is a letter written by the Apostle Paul and his young assistant, Timothy, to the Christian people living Colossae, a small city located in Asia Minor (present day Turkey). The first chapter speaks of the gift of salvation in Jesus Christ.

In your daily prayer time, please read the following:
- **Day 1** (Jeremiah 31:3 ICB) *I love you with a love that will last forever. I became your friend because of my love and kindness.*
- **Day 2** (2 Corinthians 6:16 ICB) *We are the temple of the living God! As God said, "I will live with them and walk with them. And I will be their God and they will be my people."*
- **Day 3** (Ezekiel 34:15-16 TEV) *I myself will be the shepherd of my sheep, and I will find them a place to rest. I will look for those that are lost, bring back those that wander off, bandage those that are hurt, and heal those that are sick.*
- **Day 4** (John 6:40 ICB) *(Jesus said,) "Everyone who sees the Son and believes in Him has eternal life. I will raise him up on the last day. This is what my Father wants."*
- **Day 5** (Isaiah 55:1-3 ICB) *The Lord says, "All you who are thirsty, come and drink. Those of you who do not have any money, come buy and eat! Come buy wine and milk. You don't need money; it will cost you nothing....Listen closely to me and you will eat what is good. You will enjoy food that satisfies your soul. Come to me and listen. Listen to me so you may live."*

- **Day 6** (Jeremiah 29:11-13 TEV) *The Lord says, "I alone know the plans I have for you...plans to bring about the future you hope for. Then you will call to me. You will come and pray to me, and I will answer you. You will seek me, and you will find me because you will seek me with all your heart."*
- **Day 7** (Psalms 145:17-19 ICB) *Everything the Lord does is right. With love he takes care of all He has made. The Lord is close to everyone who prays to Him....He listens when they cry and He saves them.*

God so loved the world that He sent His only Son,
that whoever believes in Him will not perish
but have eternal life.
John 3:16 NKJV

God's Love Through Jesus Christ

God loves you and me. He created us so that He could love us and so that we could choose to love Him. He wants to share His life with us and give us everything we need to have a good relationship with Him.

God's Perfect Love

How do you show other people that you love them? There are lots and lots of ways to do this. You can tell them, "I love you!" You can give them a big hug—even a big kiss. You can take care of them when they are sick or need help. You can spend time with them. You can share your very best stuff with them or give them a nice gift. When you really love someone, you want them to know it and you find a way to show them that you do.

God wants us to know that He loves us too. He says that He does, but more importantly, He shows us His love. *This is how God showed His love to us: He sent His only Son into the world to give us life through Him. True love is God's love for us, not our love for God. God sent His Son to be the way to take away our sins. That is how much God loved us!* (1 John 4:9-11 ICB).

26

When God sent His Son Jesus into the world, it was a lot more than just coming for a visit. God's Son—just like His Father—was spirit, not flesh and blood like you and me. He had to become a human being in order to come into the world. We all know the Christmas story: Jesus was born in a stable and had to be laid in a manger. It is important to remember that this little baby was really the awesome Son of God. He had lived together with His Father and the Holy Spirit in heaven before time began. He became a little baby: He couldn't feed Himself. He couldn't dress Himself. He couldn't even talk. Just becoming a human child was a really big sacrifice, but He did it because He obeyed His Father and because he loved us.

Jesus did not come simply to teach and make friends (although He did that too). He had a more important reason for coming. Jesus came to defeat sin and death: sin made it impossible for people to have a good relationship with God, and death made it impossible for people to live with Him through all eternity. Before He came into the world on Christmas morning, Jesus knew that the only thing that could really defeat sin and death was His own death upon the cross. He was willing to do whatever He had to do so that we could have a good relationship with God. Can you imagine how very much God loves us in order to send His Son into the world knowing what was going to happen to Him? When the Bible says "This is how much God loves us!" it is saying quite a lot.

We love other people, but we know that our love is not always everything it should be. Sometimes we don't treat them the way we should. Sometimes we are not as kind and generous as we should be. You probably love God, but be honest, is your love for

Him always perfect? No, it's not. No one loves God perfectly all the time. But, God's love for us is always perfect. This is why the Bible says *True love is God's love for us, not our love for God* (1 John 4:10 ICB).

God's Outrageous Love

If something is really, really unexpected, we say it is "outrageous." When God sent Jesus into the world, it was an outrageous thing to do.

Jewish people knew that God loved them because He told them He did. For thousands of years before Jesus was born, God sent messengers (called prophets) to the Jewish people and these prophets talked about God's love. In the Old Testament you can read about what the prophets said. The ancient Greek people also knew a little about God's love. They didn't have prophets like the Jewish people did, instead they had great thinkers (called philosophers) and many of them said that there was a God and that He loved the people He had made. But, if you were able to go back in time before Jesus was born and tell the Jewish or Greek people that God loved us so very much that He was going to send His only Son into the world to die for us, they would say, "That is a foolish thing to say! God would never do anything so outrageous."

Most definitely it was an outrageous thing to do and it was really, really unexpected. In his first letter to the Christians in Corinth, the Apostle Paul talks about this surprising thing Jesus had done. *We talk about Jesus on the Cross. This is a big problem for the Jews and it seems foolish to the Greeks. But Christ is the power of God to those people God has called... Even the foolishness of God is wiser than men* (1 Corinthians 1:23-25 ICB).

No one can really understand just how much God loves us. His love is more than you or I, or anyone else can understand. When the Apostle Paul wrote a letter to the Christians in Ephesus, he said that he was not praying for them to understand God's love—because no one can really understand it—but to experience His love: to know it in their hearts. *I pray that Christ will live in your hearts because of your faith...Christ's love is greater than any person can ever understand, but I pray that you will be able to know that love. Then you can be filled with the fullness of God* (Ephesians 3:17-19 ICB).

Confidence in God's Love

To be confident about something is to know that it is really, really, really true. We can be confident that God loves us because He didn't just say "I love you." He showed us His love by sending His only Son, Jesus, into the world.

One of the really wonderful things about God's love is that He didn't wait for us to be good before He loved us. It's pretty easy to love somebody when they are nice to us and when they love us first. In the Bible, however, we read that *Christ died for us...while we were still bad....God shows His great love for us in that Christ died for us while we were still sinners* (Romans 5:6&8 P). Some people think that God will not love them because they have done bad things. Of course God wants us to be good and He wants us to love Him, but even if we do bad things and don't love God the way we should, He still loves us. He loves us so much that He sent His Son to die so that we can have a good relationship with Him.

If you ever worry that God doesn't love you, just remember what He says in the Bible: *I love you with a love that lasts forever. I became your friend because of my love and kindness* (Jeremiah 31:3 ICB). In another Bible verse we read: *God says, I will never leave you; I will never forget you. So we can feel sure and say, I will not be afraid because the Lord is my helper* (Hebrews 13:5-6 ICB). Remember, you can always be confident (really, really, really sure) that God loves you and wants the very best for your life. He is your friend and His love will last forever!

Because God Loves Us, He Wants to Give Us a Gift

God loves you very much and desires to give you good things. One of the good things that He wants to give you is the Holy Spirit. The Holy Spirit is God, just like the Father is God and Jesus Christ is God. Jesus said that He would send the Holy Spirit to those who belong to Him: *When I go away I will send the Helper* (Helper is another name for the Holy Spirit.) *to you* (John 16:7 ICB). In a little while, you will have an opportunity to ask God to experience His Holy Spirit in a new way. How can you know that He wants this to happen? The answer to this question is simple: because God loves you and because God always keeps His promises!

In the Gospel of Luke, Jesus was telling His friends that He wanted them to receive the Holy Spirit. This is what He said: *If a son asks his father for bread, will his father give him a stone? Or if he asks for some fish, would any father give him a snake? Or, if your son asks for an egg, would you give him a scorpion?* (A scorpion is an insect whose sting can make people sick.) *You [fathers] know how to give good things to your children. So how much more will your Heavenly Father give the Holy Spirit to those who ask Him?* (Luke 11:11-13 P)

If you were really hungry and wanted something good to eat, who would you ask? Your Mom or Dad, right? They wouldn't give you a stone, or a snake, or a scorpion to eat, they would give you good food: a piece of bread, a tuna fish sandwich, or maybe some scrambled eggs. Your Mom and Dad love you; they want you to have the good things your body needs so that you can have a good life.

God is our Heavenly Father. No matter how good your parents are or how much they love you, God is even better than they are and loves you even more. Just like your body needs food, and clothes, and other good stuff, your spirit has needs too. One of the things your spirit needs is God's Spirit. Your spirit needs the Holy Spirit living inside of you, helping you to love God, helping you obey Him, giving you the strength you need to live for Him, giving you the "gifts of the Holy Spirit" (we will learn more about these gifts later), and helping you to become the kind of person God wants you to be.

The Bible says: *God gave his Son for us...so He will surely give us everything we need* (Romans 8:32 P). If God loves us so very much that He was willing to send His Son Jesus, we can know that God will give us His Holy Spirit. All we have to do is to ask Him: *your Heavenly Father gives the Holy Spirit to those who ask Him* (Luke 11:13 TEV).

Can Children Receive the Holy Spirit Too?

Children don't get to do everything adults do. Driving a car is an example. People have to wait until they grow up a bit before they can drive a car. Some people think that being a Christian and receiving the Holy Spirit is like that too—that it's something for adults and not for children. Do you remember when Jesus' followers tried to keep the children away from Him? Jesus said: *"Let the little children come to me. Don't stop them. The kingdom of heaven belongs to people who are like these little children"* (Mark 10:14 ICB). In another Bible verse, the Apostle Peter was talking to a large group of people. He told them that if you give your life to Jesus, *"you will receive the gift of the Holy Spirit. This promise is for you. It is also for your children"* (Acts 2:38&39 ICB).

You do not have to wait until you are a grown up to give your life to Jesus. He wants you to love Him and live for Him right now. You also do not have to wait until you are grown up to receive the Holy Spirit because the gift of the Holy Spirit is "also for children." As you get older, your relationship with Jesus can grow deeper and stronger. In the same way, you can also grow in your relationship with the Holy Spirit. One of the reasons it is important for children to receive the Holy Spirit is that He will help you grow closer to Jesus and to live more and more for Him.

When you were a baby, you drank a little bit of milk and then you were full. As you grew up, you started eating solid food—just a little bit at first and then more and more. No one would ever say, "You don't need to feed a baby until he is an adult."

Receiving the Holy Spirit is something like that. When you ask God for His Holy Spirit, He gives you just what you need. As you grow up in Christ, you can ask God for more of His Holy Spirit, and He will give you just what you need—probably more and maybe a little different than the first time you asked for the Holy Spirit. God loves you, and that is why he will always give you just what you need.

Chapter 2
Bible Readings

Over the next week, please read John 3 and Acts 2. In the third chapter of John we read about a man named Nicodemus and his conversation with Jesus Christ about salvation. In the second chapter of Acts we learn how the Holy Spirit was poured out on the first Christians during the Jewish holiday of Pentecost.

In your daily prayer time, please read the following:

- **Day 1** (Micah 4:1-2 TEV) *In days to come the mountain where the Temple stands will be the highest one of all...Many nations will come streaming to it, and their people will say, "Let us go up the hill of the Lord...He will teach us what He wants us to do; we will walk in the paths He has chosen."*
- **Day 2** (Isaiah 55:9 ICB) *Just as the heavens are higher than the earth, so my ways are higher than your ways. And my thoughts are higher than your thoughts.*
- **Day 3** (Ephesians 6:12-13 TEV) *For we are not fighting against human beings but against the wicked spiritual forces in the heavenly world....So put on God's armor now! Then...you will be able to resist the enemy's attacks.*
- **Day 4** (John 11:21-27 TEV) *Martha said to Jesus, "If You had been here, Lord, my brother would not have died! But I know that even now God will give You whatever You ask him for." Jesus said to her, "I am the resurrection and the life. Those who believe in me will live, even though they die; and those who live and believe in me will never die. Do you believe this?" "Yes, Lord!" she answered. "I do believe that You are the Christ, the Son of God, who was to come into the world."*
- **Day 5** (Romans 5:6-8 ICB) *Christ died for us while we were still weak. We were living against God, but at the right time, Christ died for us. Very few people*

will die to save the life of someone else. Although for a good person someone might possibly die. But Christ died for us while we were still sinners. In this way God shows his great love for us.

- **Day 6** (Isaiah 53:4-6 ICB) *He took our suffering on Himself and felt our pain for us....He was wounded for the wrong things we did. He was crushed for the evil things we did. The punishment, which made us well, was given to Him. And we were healed because of His wounds.*
- **Day 7** (Colossians 1:13-14 TEV) *He rescued us from the power of darkness and brought us safe into the kingdom of His dear Son, by whom we are set free.*

I came to give life—life in all its fullness.
John 10:10 ICB

The New Life

The Father Wants Everyone to Have New Life

One day Jesus told his followers, *I came to give life—life in all its fullness* (John 10:10 ICB). Some people think that being a Christian is mainly about what happens after you die. Going to heaven is really important, but Jesus wants you to experience a totally new life—His life—right now! He wants you to have the power to say "no" to sin and "yes" to what is right. He wants you to be able to pray to Him and hear His voice. And, He wants you to be filled with joy because you know Him and experience His love.

The Apostle John tells us: *This is how God shows His love for us: He sent His only Son into the world to give us life through Him...we live in God and He lives in us. We know this because God gave us His Spirit* (1 John 4:9&13 ICB). This is a really exciting idea, but what does it mean? It means a whole lot of things—far more then we have time to talk about in this little book—but it would be good right now to talk about three ways that God lives in us and we live in Him.

First, it means that we belong to God. The Bible calls Jesus the "Lord." The word Lord means that we belong to Jesus—that we should obey Him and live for Him. The Apostle Paul says: *As you received*

Jesus Christ the Lord, continue to live in Him...and have your life built on Him (Colossians 2:6&7 ICB). Christians should obey God's word and live every day of their life for Jesus. Obeying Jesus and living for Him is how we build our life on Him. It is one way we show that we belong to God and that God lives in our hearts.

Another way that God lives in us and we live in Him is that He forgives our sins. The Bible says: *If we confess our sins, He will forgive our sins...He will make us clean from all the wrong things we have done* (1 John 1:9 ICB). Because we love Jesus, we should always obey Him, but even if we disobey Him and do bad things, we can say that what we did was wrong and ask Jesus to forgive us. We have His promise that He will make us clean from all the wrong things we have done.

A third way that we live in God and He lives in us is that the Holy Spirit comes and lives inside of us. We do not know exactly how this works, but we know it happens, because Jesus said it does, and because we can experience the Holy Spirit's power at work in us. A little while before he died, Jesus told His disciples that he was going to return to His Father, and then He said something very interesting: *I will send you the Helper from the Father. He is the Spirit of Truth Who comes from the Father....It is better for you that I go away....When I go away, I will send the Helper to you...when the Spirit of truth comes He will lead you into all truth* (John 15:26, 16:7 & 16:13 ICB). Another time Jesus told His followers: *The Holy Spirit will come to you...then you will receive power* (Acts 1: 8 ICB).

God's Wonderful Promise

In the verses we just read Jesus is giving a wonderful promise: that God, the Holy Spirit, will come and live in us, that He will be our helper, He will lead us into His truth, and He will give us His power. It is wonderful for us to live in God and for Him to live in us!

Every Christian has the Holy Spirit living in them, but many Christians are not very aware of the Holy Spirit's presence or very open to His help in their life. The Apostle Paul met some people like this. We can read the story in the book of Acts. *Paul was visiting some places on the way to Ephesus. There he found some people who believed in Jesus. Paul asked them, "Did you receive the Holy Spirit when you believed?" They said, "We have never even heard of the Holy Spirit..." Then Paul laid his hands on them, and the Holy Spirit came upon them. They began speaking in tongues and prophesying* (Acts 19:1-6 ICB).

From this story we can see that it is possible to be a Christian but not really know about or experience the Holy Spirit. That is not what the Lord wants for you. He wants the Holy Spirit to make a big difference in your life. Just like Paul prayed for the people near Ephesus to experience the Holy Spirit in a new and more powerful way, people can pray with you to be more open to what the Holy Spirit wants to do in your life. We call this being baptized in the Holy Spirit.

What Does the Holy Spirit Do?

When people are baptized in the Holy Spirit, lots of changes happen. People come to know God more personally. Instead of feeling like God is far away and hard to know, they experience Him being close to them. A lot of people have trouble believing that God really loves them, but when they are baptized in the Holy Spirit, the Spirit tells them the truth: that God really does love them, that they are His precious child. The Holy Spirit also helps us make Jesus Christ the Lord of our life. He helps us to obey Jesus and live a life that pleases God.

The Holy Spirit helps to change the way we act. The Bible says: *The Spirit gives love, joy, peace, patience, kindness, goodness, faithfulness, gentleness, and self-control* (Galatians 5:22 ICB). The Lord helps us to become more and more like Him as we follow Jesus and live for Him.

We also receive a new way to worship and pray to the Lord. Do you remember what happened when the Apostle Paul prayed with the people in Ephesus to be baptized in the Holy Spirit? They started to speak in tongues. Speaking in tongues is one of the gifts of the Holy Spirit. It is the ability to speak in a language that people do not understand, but God does. The Bible says: *Those who speak in tongues are not speaking to people. They are speaking to God. No one understands them because they are speaking secret things through the Spirit* (1 Corinthians 14:2 P). Why does God want us to speak in tongues? The Bible tells us that as well: *We do not know how to pray as we should, but the Spirit Himself speaks to God for us...The Spirit speaks to God with sounds that words cannot explain...The Spirit speaks to God for His people in the way that God wants* (Romans 8: 26&27 ICB). People who speak in tongues can still pray with words that they understand, but they can also speak in tongues using words that they do not understand.

Speaking in tongues is not the only way the Holy Spirit changes the way people pray. He also helps people to praise God out loud and to thank Him for the many, many good things He does in their life. God loves it when we worship Him and praise Him. He wants us to lift up our hands when we pray (1 Timothy 2:8) and worship Him without any doubt. Sometimes it is good to pray quietly, but sometimes it is good to pray out loud, to dance and sing, and to shout our praises to God: *Be happy in the Lord and rejoice, good people. Shout for joy all you whose hearts are right!* (Psalms 32:11 P)

The Holy Spirit has many other gifts to give you. In the book of 1 Corinthians (12:7-10) there is a list of some of these gifts:
- the ability to speak words of wisdom
- the ability to speak words of knowledge
- having special faith
- praying for healing
- power to do miracles
- the ability to prophesy
- the ability to tell if evil spirits are at work
- speaking in tongues
- understanding when others speak in tongues

The Holy Spirit gives us these gifts so we can serve other people and help them grow closer to God. We should be open to all of the gifts of the Spirit and be ready to serve God wherever we are.

We have Some Work to Do.

Being baptized in the Holy Spirit is a really important step in your Christian life. It is the start of something big! With the Holy Spirit's help we can become the kind of Christian God wants us to be. While the Holy Spirit helps, we have work to do as well. We need to pray every day: worship Him, ask for His forgiveness, and ask for His help. We should also read the Bible regularly. God speaks to us through His word, and it is important for us to know what He says.

It is also important for us to build Christian friendships. We need to have people in our life that will love us, pray for us, and help us to live for Jesus. Christians call these people "brothers and sisters in Christ." It is really helpful when your parents are also your brother and sister in Christ. It is helpful when you are their brother or sister in Christ, too.

Those of us who live in a Christian community have a very special blessing from God. We are surrounded by lots and lots of Christian friends—by brothers and sisters in Christ. The children in the community are not just people who are fun to play with; they, just like you, are also growing in their love for Jesus Christ and growing in the gifts of the Holy Spirit. We can worship God together and use the gifts of the Spirit to help one another, just like the Bible says we should. The older people in the community can also help us to become better Christians. They can serve us, and we can serve them by using the gifts of the Holy Spirit. Jesus said: *I give you a new command: love each other as I have loved you. All people will know that you are my followers if you love each other* (John 13:34&35 ICB). One of the reasons your family chose to live in a Christian community is to obey Jesus' new command.

Chapter 3
Bible Readings

Over the next week, please read John 4 and Acts 13. In the fourth chapter of John we read the story of a Samaritan woman and how Jesus explained to her the gift of salvation. At the time this happened the Jews and the Samaritans would not normally speak to each other, but Jesus wanted this Samaritan woman to receive the new life He came to give. In Acts 13 we read how Paul, Barnabas, and John Mark encountered a magician named Elymas. We also read how Paul presented the Gospel of Jesus Christ to the residents of Antioch.

In your daily prayer time, please read the following:
- **Day 1** (Ezekiel 36:25-28 RSV) *I will sprinkle clean water upon you, and you will be clean...A new heart I will give you, and a new spirit I will put within you; and I will take out of you the heart of stone and give you a heart of flesh. And I will put my Spirit within you...You shall be my people, and I will be your God.*
- **Day 2** (John 14:15-18 ICB) *(Jesus said,) "If you love me, you will do the things I command. I will ask the Father and He will give you another Helper. He will give you this Helper to be with you forever. The Helper is the Spirit of Truth....He lives with you and will be in you. I will not leave you all alone."*
- **Day 3** (Acts 2:1-4 ICB) *When the day of Pentecost came, they were all together in one place. Suddenly a noise came from heaven. It sounded like a strong wind blowing. The noise filled the whole house where they were sitting. They saw something that looked like flames of fire. The flames were separated and stood over each person there. They were all filled with the Holy Spirit, and they began to speak different languages. The Holy Spirit was giving them the power to speak these languages.*

- **Day 4** (Acts 19:5-6 RSV) *On hearing this, they were baptized in the name of the Lord Jesus. And when Paul had laid his hands upon them, the Holy Spirit came on them; and they spoke with tongues and prophesied.*
- **Day 5** (Galatians 5:22-23 RSV) *The fruit of the Spirit is love, joy, peace, patience, kindness, goodness, faithfulness, gentleness, and self-control.*
- **Day 6** (1 Corinthians 12:7-11 RSV) *To each is given the manifestation of the Spirit for the common good. To one is given...wisdom, and to another... knowledge, to another faith...to another gifts of healing...to another the working of miracles, to another prophecy, to another the ability to distinguish between spirits, to another various kinds of tongues, to another the interpretation of tongues. All these are inspired by one and the same Spirit, who apportions to each one individually as he wills.*
- **Day 7** (Ephesians 2:19-22 ICB) *You are not visitors or strangers. Now you are citizens together with God's holy people. You belong to God's family. You are like a building that God owns. That building was built on the foundation of the apostles and prophets. Jesus Christ Himself is the most important stone in the building.... You are being built into a place where God lives through the Spirit.*

Chapter 4

God gives us the things we ask for.
We receive these things because we obey God's
commands, and we do what pleases Him.
1 John 3:22 ICB

Receiving God's Gift

What We Have Learned So Far

In the first chapter of this book, we learned that God loves us and has a plan for our life. He wants us to know Him, to love Him, to serve Him, and to live with Him forever. In the second chapter we learned about God's love through Jesus Christ. God created us so that He could love us and so that we could choose to love Him. He wants to share His life with us and give us everything we need to have a good relationship with Him. And in the third chapter we learned about the new life the Father wants us to have—a life in the Holy Spirit. God wants you to have the power to say "no" to sin and "yes" to what is right. He wants you to be able to pray to Him and hear His voice. And, He wants you to be filled with joy because you know Him and experience His love.

In this chapter we are going to talk about the things that we need to do so that we can be open to the Holy Spirit's work in our life.

Turning Away from the Things that Block Our Relationship with God

If we want to have a good relationship with God, we have to turn away from the things that block our relationship with Him. As we learned earlier, what blocks our relationship with God is sin—disobeying Him. So, we have to turn away from sin and start living in obedience to God. If we keep on sinning and doing what displeases God, we are not living for Him and we cannot expect to receive the good things He has for us. But, if we live for God and make Jesus the Lord of our life, then God can give us His gifts and put His life in us.

God does not want you to obey Him because you are afraid of Him or just because you want to get something from Him. He wants you to obey Him because you know that He is your Heavenly Father: because you love Him and because you respect Him. Yes, you will make mistakes and disobey Him, and when you do, you have His promise that if you repent He will forgive you and make you clean again. What He is looking for is a decision that you make in your mind and in your heart: that you will obey Him, love Him, and live for Him.

What is Repentance?

Christians use the word "repentance" to talk about turning away from what is wrong and turning towards God. The word repentance means to change direction. If you were walking down the sidewalk in one direction and turned around and started walking in the opposite direction—that would be something like repentance. It works the same way with our life. If we were living one way, doing the things we wanted to do and decided to change and start doing what God wants us to do, that would be repentance. There are several "steps" we take when we repent.

Step One: Being Honest

Repentance begins when we are honest about the bad things we have done. We tell God the things we are doing that are wrong and we tell Him that we are sorry for disobeying Him. It can be hard to be honest with God about the wrong things we have done. Even though it is hard, it is an important first step to take. Maybe it will be easier if you remember that God already knows all about it—He knows everything about you. It also helps to remember that even though you have done bad things, God still loves you, and He wants to have a good relationship with you.

Step Two: Asking for God's Help

Repenting is not an easy thing to do. If we are really going to live for Jesus and obey God's commands, we will need God's help. God is very happy to give us help. That does not mean that obeying Him will always be easy; it means that with His help we can do it if we are willing to try.

Step Three: Making a Decision

With God's help we can decide not to do the things which displease Him. It does not matter what we have done in the past— disobeying our parents, cheating at school, saying unkind things to people, lying, and even worse things—we can say, "I am not going to do that any more; I am going to obey God and do what is right."

Step Four: Asking for Forgiveness

We also need to ask God for forgiveness. When we do wrong things, we are not loving God and respecting Him the way that we should. So we go to Him in prayer and say: "I am sorry for the wrong things I have done, please forgive me." And God will forgive us: He will make us clean, and He will not even remember the bad things we have done. In the book of Psalms it says: *So great is His love for those who respect Him, He has taken our sins away from us—as far as the east is from the west* (Psalms 103:11&12 ICB). In the book of Hebrews it says: *I will forgive them for the wrong things they have done. I will not remember their sins any more* (Hebrews 8:12 P).

We Must Ask In Faith

There are two kinds of faith. The first kind of faith is what we believe about God—it is called "believing faith." We believe, for example, that God exists; that God is three persons: the Father, the Son, and the Holy Spirit; we believe that Jesus is fully and completely God and also fully and completely human—just like you and me.

The second kind of faith is trusting that God will do what He says He will do—it is called "trusting faith." This kind of faith means that we believe that God loves us, that He has the power to do what we ask, and that He really wants to give us the good things He has for us.

God wants us to have the second kind of faith when we ask Him for something. There is a story in the Gospel of Matthew that teaches us about trusting faith. One day Jesus told His followers to get into a boat and travel to the other side of a big lake. Jesus went away to pray. That night a big storm came up. The wind and the waves tossed the little boat and the disciples were afraid. Early in the morning Jesus came to the boat walking on the water. He said: "Have courage!" Peter said: "Lord, if that is really you, tell me to come to you walking on the water." Jesus said, "Come." So, Peter got out of the boat and he was walking on the water—just like Jesus. But, Peter started to look down at the water. He saw the wind and the waves and he became afraid. All of a sudden he started to sink, so Jesus reached out and saved him. Jesus asked Peter, "Why did you doubt?"

Peter started his walk with trusting faith: his eyes were on Jesus and he remembered that Jesus had told him to come. It was when he took his eyes off Jesus and started looking at the wind, the waves, and the water, that trusting faith left Him and he started to doubt.

We need to rely on what God has said. He said that He wants to give the Holy Spirit to those who ask for it. We can believe what God says because God does not lie. If God promises something and we ask for it, we can expect that it will happen. It might not happen just the way we expect, but God will respond when His children ask. Jesus talks about trusting faith in the Gospel of Luke: *Ask and God will give to you. Search and you will find. Knock and the door will*

*open for you... What would you fathers do if your son
asks for an egg, would you give him a scorpion? Even
though you are bad, you know how to give good things
to your children. Surely your Heavenly Father knows
how to give the Holy Spirit to those who ask Him*
(Luke 11:9-13 ICB).

Prayer to Be Baptized in the Holy Spirit

Soon you will be prayed with to be baptized in
the Holy Spirit. If this is the first time for you to be
prayed with to be baptized in the Holy Spirit, you can
expect to experience the Holy Spirit in a new way. If
you have been prayed with before, you can ask to receive a gift of the Holy Spirit that you have not experienced before, or you can ask to grow in a gift that
you already have. The Apostle Paul told his young
friend Timothy to do this. *Remember to stir up,* Paul
said, *the gift God gave you. God gave you that gift
when I laid my hands on you. Now let it grow, as a
small flame grows into a fire* (2 Timothy 1:6 ICB). So,
even if you have already been baptized in the Holy
Spirit, even if you have already received a gift of the
Spirit—or two, or three—you can always grow in your
relationship with the Lord and in the gifts and the
fruit of the Holy Spirit.

Did you notice that the Apostle Paul said that
he "laid his hands" on Timothy? That is how we pray
for people to be baptized in the Holy Spirit: we put
our hands on them and pray to God to pour His Holy
Spirit on them. God often includes other people when
He does a special work in a person's life. These other
people can be your own parents, your own brothers
and sisters, friends of your family, or your brothers
and sisters in Christ—young ones and older ones.
The Holy Spirit comes from God, not from people's

hands, but by having people put their hands on you, God includes other Christians in this—His special work in your life.

What is Going to Happen?

What happens to you will be just what happened to the first Christians. We can read about the very first time people were baptized in the Holy Spirit in the book of Acts: *They were all filled with the Holy Spirit and they began to speak in tongues* (Acts 2:4 ICB). God filled these Christians with His Holy Spirit. Only God can give His Holy Spirit to you. We know that He will do this, because He says if you ask for the Holy Spirit, He will give the Holy Spirit to you. Did you notice in the verse above that everyone received the Holy Spirit? God did not give His Spirit to only a few people; He gave the Holy Spirit to everyone. You can trust that God will give His Holy Spirit to you, just like He has given His Spirit to lots and lots of other people.

God gave His Spirit, but the people did something too: they began to speak in tongues. God did not move their mouths for them; each person had to begin speaking. Perhaps they were a little unsure of themselves at first, but they did it anyway. They began speaking with trusting faith that the Holy Spirit would turn what they said into a special language that no one else can understand (1 Corinthians 14:2).

Each person's experience of being baptized in the Spirit is a little different. Some people get really excited, others remain calm. Some people are filled with God's joy, others are not. Some people start speaking in tongues right away; others receive a prophecy from God and for others, these gifts come a little later. It is important to be open to whatever God wants to do in your life. This is a way of saying, "Lord, I trust You to give me what I need right now. Whatever You have for me, my answer is 'Yes.'"

Things That Get in the Way

Imagine that someone gives you a present in a box wrapped with colorful paper. If you refused to take off the wrapping paper and open the box, this would keep you from enjoying the present. Sometimes people act the same way with God's gift of the Holy Spirit.

Some people think, "I am not worthy to receive God's Spirit." Well, that is true—no one is worthy, but God gives His Spirit anyway. Actually, you already have the Holy Spirit in you. You are going to be prayed with to open up to more of the Holy Spirit's work in your life. That is always a good thing to do.

Some people are afraid that they will look silly. A long time ago King David was filled with the Holy Spirit and he started dancing (2 Samuel 6:14). Saul's daughter, Michal, thought he looked silly and told him so. But, David did not care. He was happy to do whatever God wanted him to do—even if it made him look silly.

Some people think that when the Holy Spirit comes into them, that He will take over and they will lose control of themselves. Remember, the Holy Spirit is in you right now, but you still control what you do. Also, the Bible says that you stay in control: *The spirits of the prophets are under the control of the proph-*

ets themselves. God is not a God of confusion but a God of peace (1 Corinthians 14:32&33 ICB)

We do not have to be afraid of what God wants to do in our life. He loves us, and he will always do what is best for us!

Chapter 4
Bible Readings

Over the next week, please read John 14 and Acts 8. In John 14, Jesus tells His followers that He is going to prepare a heavenly home for them, and that He will send the Holy Spirit who will reveal the truth to them. In Acts 8 we read about Paul before he became a Christian. In those days he was known by the name of Saul. We also read how receiving the Holy Spirit had such a powerful impact, that a magician named Simon offered money so he could have this power too. Finally, we read about an Ethiopian official who believed in Jesus Christ.

In your daily prayer time, please read the following:
- **Day 1** (Titus 3:4-6 TEV) *But when the kindness and love of God our Savior was revealed, He saved us. It was not because of any good deeds that we ourselves had done, but because of His own mercy that He saved us, through the Holy Spirit, who gives us new birth and new life by washing us. God poured the Holy Spirit abundantly on us through Jesus Christ our Savior.*
- **Day 2** (John 7:37-38 ICB/RSV) *Jesus stood up and said in a loud voice, "If anyone is thirsty, let him come to me and drink. If a person believes in me, rivers of living water will flow out from his heart. This is what the Scripture says." Now this He said about the Spirit, which those who believed in Him were to receive.*
- **Day 3** (Mark 1:14-15 ICB) *Jesus went to Galilee and preached the Good News from God. Jesus said, "The right time has come. The Kingdom of God is near! Change your hearts and lives and believe the Good News!"*
- **Day 4** (Acts 2:38-39 ICB) *Peter said to them, "Change your hearts and lives and be baptized, each one of you, in the name of Jesus Christ....And you*

will receive the gift of the Holy Spirit. This promise is for you. It is also for your children. It is for everyone the Lord our God calls to Himself."

- **Day 5** (2 Peter 1:5-8 ICB) *Try as much as you can to add these things to your lives: to your faith, add goodness; and to your goodness, add knowledge; and to your knowledge, add self-control; and to your self-control, add the ability to hold on; and to your ability to hold on, add service for God; and to your service for God, add kindness to your brothers and sisters in Christ; and to this kindness, add love. If all these things are in you and you are growing....They will help your knowledge of our Lord Jesus Christ make your lives better.*

- **Day 6** (Romans 4:20-21 ICB) *He never doubted that God would keep his promise. Abraham never stopped believing. He grew stronger in his faith and gave praise to God. Abraham was sure that God was able to do the thing that God promised.*

- **Day 7** (Luke 11:9-13 ICB) (Jesus said,) *"Continue to ask, and God will give to you. Continue to search, and you will find. Continue to knock, and the door will open for you. Yes, if a person continues asking, he will receive. If he continues searching, he will find. And if he continues knocking, the door will open for him. What would you fathers do if your son asks for a fish? Would any of you give him a snake? Or if your son asks for an egg, would you give him a scorpion? You know how to give good things to your children. So surely your Heavenly Father knows how to give the Holy Spirit to those who ask Him."*

Note to Moms and Dads: *This is the chapter that deals with the prayer session. You will want to make this an event for your child. If you have family friends with children who are already baptized in the Spirit, invite them to be a part of the prayer session. It can really help your child to have someone close to his or her age participate in the prayer time. When Jan and I prayed with our children to be baptized in the Holy Spirit, we invited another community family to share the Lord's Day meal with us and had the prayer time after dinner. This always created a nice atmosphere.*

Read the following chapter ahead of time. Notice the elements mentioned for the prayer session:

- *opening prayer and worship*
- *the prayer of commitment*
- *taking authority over the evil one*
- *praying for the baptism of the Holy Spirit*
- *praying for the gift of tongues*
- *closing prayer and worship*

It is a good idea to read this chapter to your child a few days before the prayer session. Ask them clearly if they understand what it means to commit their life to Jesus. Ask them if that is what they really want to do. If the child has already been baptized, the prayer of commitment will be very similar to the commitment made at their baptism. It is important for them to embrace that commitment and make it their own. If your child has not been baptized, if they understand the commitment, and they really want to make it—now would probably be a good time to arrange for them to be baptized. If, however, they do not have a basic understanding or do not want to make such a commitment, it would be best to put being bap-

tized in the Spirit on hold and work on the more pressing issue of their relationship with Jesus Christ.

As for speaking in tongues, this book takes the approach of encouraging without pressuring. This is, I think, a good approach for Mom and Dad to take as well. We would have greater expectation that an adult would speak in tongues right away. It is not uncommon for children to experience the gifts more gradually. If the child does not want to speak in tongues, talk with them about why not. Explain that it is an important gift and a good gift—a gift that God might want them to have. If they want to have the gift but it does not come right away, encourage them to keep seeking the gift and it will come eventually. If, down the road, you think they might be ready, you can always pray over them again. As explained in the introduction, it is good to pray for people with some regularity.

Chapter 5

The Holy Spirit will come to you,
and you will receive power.
Acts 1:8 ICB

Being Baptized in the Spirit

This chapter is different from the others: there will be less reading and talking, and more action. This chapter talks about the time when you will be prayed with to be baptized in the Holy Spirit. Remember what Jesus said in the Gospel of Luke: *Surely your Heavenly Father knows how to give the Holy Spirit to those who ask Him* (Luke 11:13 ICB). That is exactly what will happen now.

The prayer time will begin with a time of worshipping the Lord. It is always good to start big steps (little steps too) by worshiping our God who made us to know Him, to love Him, to serve Him, and to live with Him through all time. With your family and friends you can say that the Lord is your God. Next, you are going to say a prayer. This is a special prayer where you say out loud that you want to live your life for Jesus Christ: that you will not follow Satan but you will obey and follow Jesus. We call this a "prayer of commitment." A commitment is a promise that you make to someone else. You should only make this promise if that is what you really want to do. You might have made a promise similar to this one in the past. If you have, this promise is just a way of saying, "Jesus, I <u>still</u> want to follow You, live for You, and obey You."

Next, the people who are praying for you will tell Satan that you belong to Jesus. They will say that Satan can not do any work in your life and he must leave you alone. When they order Satan to go away, they will use the name of Jesus. Satan always has to obey Jesus, because Jesus is God and Satan is not. You should tell Satan that he has to go away from you too. When you do, you should also use the name of Jesus. The Bible says that Satan is a liar. He may try to tell you that you will not really be baptized in the Spirit, that God does not really love you, or that you will not be able to speak in tongues. If those lies come into your head, you can tell him just what the Bible says: *Your Heavenly father knows how to give me the Holy Spirit when I ask Him* (Luke 11:13 ICB).

When this is done, people will put their hands on your head or shoulders and ask God to baptize you in His Holy Spirit. Everyone is a little different and what they feel and experience when this happens is a little different too. You should not expect to feel a certain way. Just turn your mind and heart to the Lord and receive from Him whatever he wants to give you.

Most people speak in tongues when they are baptized in the Spirit: not always right away, but this is a gift God wants to give you so you can use it to pray to Him and grow closer to Him. This is just what happened to the early Christians in the book of Acts: *They were all filled with the Holy Spirit, and they began to speak in tongues* (Acts 2:4 ICB). You should not tell the Lord that you do not want the gift of tongues; instead you should say, "Lord, whatever You want to give me, that is what I want to have." So, after you have asked to be baptized in the Holy Spirit, ask to receive the gift of tongues as well, and then start making sounds. You can have trusting faith that the Holy Spirit will turn those sounds into a language that no one can understand (not even you) except God. Do not be afraid if what comes out of your mouth sounds like baby talk. Babies learn how to speak English by making their baby noises. That is how most people learn to speak in tongues too. Do not worry about the sounds; instead keep your mind and your heart focused on the Lord.

Once in a while people receive a prophecy when they are baptized in the Spirit. If the Lord puts words in your mind, go ahead and speak them out loud. Sometimes the Lord gives people a prayer that they can pray out loud. If that happens, go ahead and pray that prayer out loud. Some of the people who are praying with you may have a prophecy or a special prayer for you. You can also experience the Lord by listening to what He says through other people.

There will also be a time to worship God at the end. Now that you are baptized in the Spirit, you will have a new power from God to worship Him. Pray out loud, raise your hands, feel free to dance or jump up and down, speak in tongues, and remember to say thank you to God. It is always good to say thank you when someone gives you a present, and that is just what God has done for you!

Prayer of Commitment

Here is the prayer of commitment to Jesus Christ.

Leader: Do you say no to Satan and the wrong things he wants you to do?

You: Yes I do.

Leader: Do you believe that Jesus is the Son of God, that He died to take away your sins, and that He rose from the dead so that you can live with Him forever?

You;   Yes I do.

Leader: Will you follow Jesus as your Savior and as your Lord?

You: Yes I will.
            Lord Jesus Christ, I want to belong to you from now on. I want to be free from Satan and I will not follow him. I want to live in Your kingdom and be part of Your people. I ask You to forgive the bad things I have done, and I will try not to sin any more. I give my life to You, and I promise to obey You as my Lord. I ask you to baptize me in the Holy Spirit.

After the Prayer Time

During the prayer time, you might have had some different feelings. Maybe you did not. Remember, you did not ask for feelings but for the Holy Spirit. Feelings are not important, but having God at work in new ways inside of you is important. You were baptized in the Holy Spirit, because that is what God promises to do when you ask Him. Now that God is at work in you in a new way, you can expect to have His power when you pray, when you read the Bible, and as you live for Him every day.

If you did not speak in tongues, do not worry about it. Expect this gift to come soon. When you pray this coming week, give lots of time to praise and thanking the Lord. Do this out loud and you may discover that you can speak in tongues. Even if you do not speak in tongues right away, remember to thank Him for what He has given to you and to praise Him every day. You can always ask to receive the gift of tongues at a later time.

You told Satan to go away, but he may still have some lies to tell you. He will try to rob you of this gift from God. He might tell you that you were not really baptized in the Spirit, that you did not really speak in tongues, or that all of this stuff is just silly. Remember: God made a promise, you asked to be baptized in the Holy Spirit, and so you are. Tell Satan to take a hike!

You can not expect that all of your problems will go away now that you are baptized in the Spirit. The Bible says that God uses the problems in our life to help us grow stronger and closer to Him: *We have joy when trouble comes, because we know that these troubles produce patience, and patience produces character, and character produces hope. This hope will never disappoint us because God has poured His love into our hearts. God gave us His love through the Holy Spirit, Who was given to us* (Romans 5:3-5 ICB). Even if problems keep coming, now you have a new power in the Holy Spirit to work them out.

Remember to pray every day. Spend time with God, worship Him, thank Him, and tell Him that you love Him. Go ahead and pray out loud and use your voice to give God glory. Also, speak in tongues when you pray. Even though you do not understand the words, God does, because the Holy Spirit is praying to Him through this gift. You should also read some of the Bible in your prayer time. God will speak to you through His word. Jesus wants His servants to be faithful. He told a story about a servant who did what he should: *You did well*, the master told him. *You are a good servant who can be trusted. You did well with small things, so I will let you care for bigger things. Come and share my happiness with me* (Matthew 25:21 ICB). Like the servant, we should be faithful too, and we can start by being faithful to our daily prayer time.

If your family is part of a community, make sure you go to the community gathering with your parents. Now that you are baptized in the Holy Spirit, you can praise the Lord out loud with all of your adult brothers and sisters in Christ and with your young brothers and sisters in Christ too. You can speak in tongues during the prayer meeting, and sing in tongues as well. Community meetings are a lot more fun when you can participate in what is going on.

Chapter 5
Bible Readings

Over the next week, please read John 15 and Galatians 5. In John 15 we read Jesus' teaching about how we should abide in Him and how He abides in us. (The word "abide" means to live with; so Jesus comes and lives with you and you get to live with Him.) It is a powerful passage and can be life-changing. In Galatians 5, the Apostle Paul teaches about how we are made right with God by His grace, by our union with Jesus Christ, and by following the guiding of the Holy Spirit.

In your daily prayer time, please read the following:
- **Day 1** (1Corinthians 14:15 RSV) *I will pray with the spirit and I will pray with the mind also; I will sing with the spirit and I will sing with the mind also.*
- **Day 2** (Matthew 25:23 TEV) *His master said to him, 'Well done, good and faithful servant; you have been faithful over a little, I will set you over much; enter into the joy of your master.'*
- **Day 3** (Ephesians 6:18 ICB) *Pray in the Spirit at all times. Pray with all kinds of prayers, and ask for everything you need. To do this you must always be ready. Never give up. Always pray for all God's people.*
- **Day 4** (Romans 8:5-6 TEV) *Those who live as their human nature tells them to, have their minds controlled by what human nature wants. Those who live as the Spirit tells them to, have their minds controlled by what the Spirit wants....To be controlled by the Spirit results in life and peace.*
- **Day 5** (1 Corinthians 14:1 ICB) *Love, then, is what you should try for. And you should truly want to have the spiritual gifts. The gift you should want most is to be able to prophesy.*
- **Day 6** (Jude 1:20-21 ICB) *Use your most holy faith to build yourselves up strong. Pray with the Holy Spirit.*

63

Keep yourselves in God's love. Wait for the Lord Jesus Christ with his mercy to give you life forever.

- **Day 7** (Rom 12:11 RSV) *Never flag in zeal, be aglow with the Spirit, serve the Lord.*

Note to Moms and Dads: *If your child is going to become a mature Christian, he or she will need to develop some basic Christian disciplines. Adults and children mostly need the same things to be strong and healthy physically, but children often need smaller portions. The same principle applies to our children's spiritual lives: they need the same things that you do, but they will normally take smaller portions. Take prayer, for example. If a child prays just five or ten minutes a day, this is astounding—and it will bear tremendous fruit in their life over time. They can pray longer as they mature. The important thing to learn now is the daily discipline—making sure that time is given to God each and every day.*

Many parents find it helpful to have their child join them for personal prayer once in a while. In this way the child can learn by seeing and by doing. You will probably need to explain what you are doing: "I'm going to spend time praising God for a while; why don't you join me." You will want to make sure that you adjust the time you spend praying to your child's capacity. Also, help them to find a good time to pray and then ask them if they are doing what they decided to do. Preferably they should try to pray around the same time every day—especially week days. That is a good technique for building a habit.

The "wheel diagram" has been a powerful tool in the lives of many, many Christians. Even so, it has some shortcomings. A common criticism from some Christians is that it does not include the sacraments. There are three common ways of dealing with this critique. (1) Recognize the disciplines listed on the diagram as personal disciplines, administered by the individual, not services or sacraments administered by the church. (2) Add additional spokes for attending church, receiving the sacraments, giving alms, fasting, and the like. (3) Make the existing spokes "wide" enough to accommodate additional material. Community, for example, can also include attending church and receiving communion. Service can include giving alms.

I have kept the diagram and the explanation of it simple so that it works well for an ecumenical audience. If you are uncomfortable presenting it as is, feel free to make modifications that work better for your church tradition.

Chapter 6

I am the vine, and you are the branches.
If a person remains in me and I remain in him,
then he produces much fruit.
Without me he can do nothing.
John 15:5 ICB

Growing in the Lord

Being baptized in the Spirit is an exciting step. The Holy Spirit gave you His power and His gifts and this is really important. Now you have an important job to do: to grow spiritually—to grow in your relationship with Jesus and to grow in the life of the Holy Spirit.

Staying Connected to Jesus Christ

Children grow physically. They start as little babies and over time they become grown up. In order to grow up well, people need to do some important things. People need to eat, they need to get some exercise, they need to go to school, and they need to get enough sleep. If any of these important things are missing, people do not grow up as well as they should—in fact, they might even die.

Spiritual growth is like physical growth in this way. In order to grow spiritually, people need to do some important things. Four very important things that Christians need to do to grow spiritually are these: pray every day, read the Bible, serve Jesus, and live in Christian community. Doing these things help keep you connected to Jesus Christ.

Jesus said: *I am the vine, and you are the branches. If a person remains in me and I remain in him, then he produces much fruit* (John 15:5 ICB). If you cut a branch off from a tomato plant, that branch would not continue to grow and it would not produce a tomato; it would wither up and die. In order to keep growing and producing fruit, tomato branches need to stay connected to tomato vines. Your Christian life is like that tomato branch. If you want to keep growing and to become the kind of person God wants you to be, you need to stay connected to Jesus Christ. Praying, reading the Bible, serving Jesus, and living in community helps you keeping connected to Jesus.

There is a picture we use to help explain the things we should do to stay connected to Jesus, we call it the wheel diagram.

As you can see, the wheel diagram looks like an old-fashioned wagon wheel. At the very center of the wheel is a cross. The cross stands for Jesus. Jesus should be at the very center of our life because He is our Lord: we belong to Him and live for Him. On the outside is the rim of the wheel. This stands for your Christian life. The things that connect the rim, your Christian life, to Jesus Christ are called spokes, and each spoke has a label: prayer, scripture, service, and community.

Many people find this a helpful picture to keep in their mind. If their Christian life is not working well, they can remember the spokes and ask themselves: "Am I praying every day? Am I reading the Bible? Am I serving Jesus as I should? Do I live in community with other Christians?" If the answer to any of these questions is "NO" the person knows what to work on, so that his or her Christian life stays well connected to Jesus.

Praying Every Day

Friendships grow when we spend time with people. We talk to them about what is important to them and what is important to us. Jesus wants to be your friend. If you want that friendship to grow, you need to make spending time with Him part of your everyday life. When Jesus taught people about praying, He said: *When you pray, you should go into your room and close the door. Then pray to your Father who cannot be seen. Your Father can see what you do in secret, and He will reward you* (Matthew 6:6 ICB). This verse contains lots of important information. We should look at it closely.

Jesus said, "When you pray." He did not say, "If you pray." This is important. Praying is an important thing to do, so we need to make sure that we do it—every day. Praying is not always easy. Sometimes it is a hard thing to do. We might feel bad about the bad things we have done, we might be really, really busy, or we might just feel a little lazy. One of the important things Christians need to learn is that we will not always feel like doing the things we should, but we do them anyway because we want to be obedient and we want to stay connected to Jesus. You have to brush your teeth a couple of times every day. You might not always want to brush your teeth, but you know that if you do not, you will get cavities. So, every morning and every evening (and maybe a couple more times besides) you brush your teeth. Praying is a little like brushing your teeth: it is something that you do every day. You should pray even if you do not feel much like praying.

"When you pray," Jesus said, "go into your room and close the door." This does not mean that you have to go into your bedroom, but it is good to have a place where you can pray: a place where you will not be distracted or interrupted. For example, it would be really hard to pray in a room where other people are watching television. Pretty quickly, you would stop praying and start watching television. Instead, find a place where you can pay attention to God: where you can talk to Him and He can talk to you.

Jesus also mentioned a special challenge for some people: *Pray to your Father who cannot be seen.* Some people find it hard to talk to someone they cannot see. When you think about it, however, this is something you do all the time. When you talk on the telephone, you are talking to someone you cannot see. Talking on the telephone seems pretty normal, and talking to God can be pretty normal too—it just takes a little practice. Many Christians find it helpful to pray out loud. Praying out loud helps you to think about what you are saying and not get distracted. Yes, God knows what you are thinking, but it can help you if you pray out loud.

Finally, Jesus says that His Father will reward people who pray. A very important reward for praying every day is that we get to spend time with God and by doing so we grow closer to Him and stay connected to Him. Some people pray for a few minutes; others pray much, much longer. If you can only pray for five or ten minutes a day, that is what you should do. Remember, though, to pray every day.

How to Pray

Many, many books have been written about how to pray. Lots of people in our communities have found the following way helpful.

1. Praise the Lord

Start with a time of praise. Tell the Lord how wonderful He is. Raise your hands to Him and shout your praise to Him; you can even dance if you want to. If you received the gift of tongues, spend some time praying in tongues. Remember, speaking in tongues allows the Holy Spirit to pray through you.

2. Confess and Ask Forgiveness for Sin

Do you remember what the Bible says about confessing sin? It says: *If we confess our sins, He will forgive our sins...He will make us clean from all the wrong things we have done* (1 John 1:9 ICB) So spend some time telling Jesus about the wrong things you have done; tell Him that you are truly sorry, and ask His forgiveness. We can also ask Jesus to help us stop doing the bad things that we do.

3. Thank God for His Blessings

The Lord has given you many wonderful gifts: your life, your health, your home and family, His salvation, the gift of the Holy Spirit, His forgiveness, and lots of other blessings. Spend some time every day thanking God for all of His gifts. After a while you may notice that you are thanking Him for the same things day after day. That is OK because the Lord gives you many of the same blessings every day, but you can also use your imagination and think of new things for which to thank Him.

4. Pray for Yourself and for Other People

The Apostle Paul and his young friend Timothy wrote a letter to the Christians who lived in Philippi. They told them: *Do not worry about anything, but pray and ask God for everything you need...And God's peace will keep your hearts and minds in Christ Jesus* (Philippians 4:6&7 ICB). The Lord has given you a special gift: you can go to Him with your problems and with your cares. You may not get everything that you ask for, but you can have trusting faith that God will always do what is best. You do not have to spend time worrying about things. Instead, you can spend your time growing closer to Jesus.

Reading Your Bible

It is important to read your Bible regularly. Many Christians spend time reading the Bible during their prayer time, some Christians find another time when they can read their Bible. It is important for you to find a good time when you can read your Bible, and then make a decision to read it regularly.

The Bible is not like other books. It is a special book because it contains the word of God. In the book of Hebrews it says, *God's word is alive and powerful...God's word can tell what is going on in our heart and in our feelings* (Hebrews 4:12 P). God will speak to you through His word. He will tell you about Himself, and He will tell you what He wants those who follow Him to be doing.

Jesus told people: *Blessed* (the word "blessed" means that a person is happy and doing well) *are those who hear the word of God and obey it* (Luke 11:28 NKJV). If you want to be blessed by God, then read His word and obey what it says.

We have not yet talked about the other two spokes: service and community. The next chapter will cover these important things.

Chapter 6
Bible Readings

Over the next week, please read John 17 and Philippians 3. John 17 contains Jesus' final prayer before His crucifixion. What was on His heart at this important moment? You were—and He prayed for you. In Philippians 3, Paul speaks about his former life, which he compares to garbage, and the new life that he found in Jesus Christ.

In your daily prayer time, please read the following:

- **Day 1** (John 4:14 ICB) *"Whoever drinks this water will be thirsty again. But whoever drinks the water I give will never be thirsty again. The water I give will become a spring of water flowing inside him. It will give eternal life."*
- **Day 2** (John 15:5 TEV) *I am the vine, and you are the branches. Those who remain in me, and I in them, will bear much fruit; for you can do nothing without me.*
- **Day 3** (Ephesians 4:23-24 RSV) *Be renewed in the spirit of your minds, and put on the new nature, created after the likeness of God in true righteousness and holiness.*
- **Day 4** (Luke 5:15-16 ICB) *The news about Jesus was spreading more and more. Many people came to hear Jesus and be healed of their sicknesses. But Jesus often slipped away to other places to be alone so that he could pray.*
- **Day 5** (2 Timothy 3:15-17 ICB) *The Scriptures (the Bible) are able to make you wise. And that wisdom leads to salvation through faith in Christ Jesus. All Scripture is inspired by God and is useful for teaching and showing people what is wrong with their lives. It is useful for correcting faults and teaching how to live right. Using the Scriptures, the person who serves*

God will be ready and will have everything he needs to do every good work.

- **Day 6** (Acts 2:41-47 TEV) *Many of them believed and were baptized, and about three thousand people were added that day. They spent their time in learning from the apostles, taking part in the fellowship, and sharing in the fellowship meals and the prayers....All the believers continued together in close fellowship and shared their belongings with one another....Day after day they met as a group in the Temple, and they had their meals together in their homes, eating with glad and humble hearts, (and) praising God.*

- **Day 7** (Colossians 4:5-6 ICB) *Be wise in the way you act with people who are not believers. Use your time the best way you can. When you talk, you should always be kind and wise. Then you will be able to answer everyone in the way you should.*

*I am not yet everything God wants me to be,
but I keep trying to reach that goal
because Jesus has made me His own.*
Philippians 3:12 P

Living for Jesus

In the last chapter we looked at the wheel diagram. Let us look at it again to help us remember.

Jesus Christ is the hub: the very center of the wheel. The rim is your Christian life, and the spokes are the different things you do that connect you to Jesus. In this diagram the spokes represent praying every day, reading the Bible regularly, serving the Lord and other people, and living in Christian community. In the last chapter we talked about daily prayer and reading the Bible. In this chapter we will talk a bit about service and community.

Serving Jesus and Serving Others

Just before Jesus died he had a special meal with His disciples. At the end of the meal Jesus took a towel and a bowl full of water. He went to each of His disciples and washed their feet. Imagine how dirty those feet must have been. This was long before shoes and socks were worn; people just wore open sandals. There were no sidewalks either; people walked in the mud and the dust. Those feet would have been filthy. Washing them would be a dirty job.

Jesus was the most important person in that room. He was God's own Son. He was also the teacher and the master of His disciples. It was odd that Jesus was the one to wash each person's feet. When Peter saw what Jesus was doing, he said, "No! You will never wash my feet." But, Jesus insisted, so even Peter's feet were washed by the Lord. When He finished the job, Jesus spoke to His disciples: *I, your Lord and Teacher have washed your feet. So you should wash each other's feet. I did this as an example for you, so you should do as I have done...you will be blessed if you do this* (John 13:14-17 ICB).

If we really want to become like Jesus, we have to serve other people—because that is what Jesus did. Some people may think that only grownups serve and not children. If you are going to live for Jesus, if you want to become like Him—then you need to follow His example. There are lots of ways that children can serve Jesus by serving others; in fact you can serve Him without even leaving home. You can serve by doing your chores, by doing them well, by doing them with a smile on your face, and by doing them without being reminded.

You can also look around for jobs that you can do. Every one of the disciples could have noticed the dirty feet. They could have said, "Hey guys, you all have dirty feet. Let me wash them for you." If servants of the Lord just keep looking for ways to serve others, there will be no lack of work for them to do. At our community center, a group of children picked up all the litter that had collected over the winter. Another group of kids came with their dad to rake the leaves and trim the bushes. These young people were being like Jesus, they looked for what needed to be done, and they did it.

Another way you can serve other people is by being open to using the gifts of the Holy Spirit that you have received to help other people. This is what the Bible says: *The gifts of the Spirit are given to each one for the benefit of all* (1 Corinthians 12:7 P). So, if you are at a prayer meeting and you receive a prophecy or a scripture to read out loud—be bold and tell others what the Lord has given you to share. If someone is sick, you can pray for them to be healed. When it is time to worship the Lord, you can help the prayer meeting be better for everyone by worshiping God enthusiastically. The Lord has given you the Holy Spirit, not just so you can grow closer to Him, but so that other people can grow closer to Him as well.

Living in Community

This book was written for people who live in Christian communities, so you probably already know a lot about living in community. Christian community happens when people who love Jesus and have given their lives to Him, decide to help each other live for Jesus in a really good way. There are lots and lots of Christian communities around the world. Sometimes Christian communities are formed in a local church or parish. Some Christian communities are just for single men or for single women. Sometimes, however, the Lord forms a Christian community from people who attend different churches or parishes, and sometimes he makes communities of families and single people together. No matter who makes up the community, the most important thing is that the members of the community have really given their lives to Jesus and are actually helping one another live for Jesus in a really good way.

The first Christian community was formed right after the very first Christians were baptized in the Holy Spirit. We can read about this in the book of Acts: *They spent their time learning the apostles' teaching, they continued to share their lives with one another, to break bread, and to pray...They divided their money and gave it to those people who needed it* (Acts 2:42&45 P). I hope you noticed how similar this list of what the first Christians did is to the wheel diagram: they prayed, they learned the apostles' teaching (today we read the Bible to do this), they served others by giving them money, and they shared their lives together—and that is community.

The Christian life is not something you are supposed to do all by yourself. Other people should

80

be there to help you and you should be there to help other people. When we become God's children, He wants us to love and take good care of all of our brothers and sisters in Christ. The Apostle John said: *This is how we know what real love is: Jesus gave His life for us, so we should give our lives for our brothers and sisters* (1 John 3:16 ICB). You are blessed (Do you remember that "blessed" means that a person is happy and doing well?) to be living your life in a Christian community. You have to be careful, though, because it is not enough that your parents are members of a Christian community. If you really want to live in Christian community, you have to give your life to Jesus as best as you are able and help the other people in community live for Him in a really good way.

Dealing with Trouble

Some people think that once they give their life to Jesus, all their troubles will go away. You need to understand, that this is not the way things work. Jesus said: *In this world you will have trouble, but be brave! I have victory over the world* (John 16:33 P). Jesus did not say that we will always get everything we want; He did not promise that things would always go our way. What He did promise is that He will always be with us: *You can be sure,* Jesus said, *I will be with you always. I will continue with you to the end of the world* (Matthew 28:20 ICB).

I am sure you know that Jesus had troubles in His life, just as you will have troubles too. The Lord uses the troubles in your life to help you grow more like Him. We read about how God uses the troubles in life in the book of James: *Consider yourself fortunate when all kinds of troubles come your way. You know that these things are testing your faith, and this will help you grow in patience* (James 1:2&3 P). So, even when you are having trouble—even when you are having really, really bad trouble—you can know that God is right there with you and that He is using the trouble to make you a stronger Christian. The Apostle Paul said: *We know that in everything God works for the good of those who love Him* (Romans 8:28 ICB).

The Bible says that no matter what is going on in our life—whether it is good or bad—we should be thankful to God and give Him praise: *Be full of joy always and pray at all times. Be thankful in all circumstances. This is God's will for you in Christ Jesus* (1 Thessalonians 5:16-18 TEV). This advice is good when our life is hard; it is also good advice when everything is going just the way we want. No matter what is happening, Christians should always be full of joy, we should always be praying, and we should always be giving God our thanks!

Chapter 7
Bible Readings

Over the next week, please read John 20 and Revelation 21. In John 20 we read the story of Jesus appearing to his disciples immediately after His rising from the dead. Revelation 21 offers a description of the heavenly home that Jesus Christ has prepared for those who belong to Him.

In your daily prayer time, please read the following:

- **Day 1** (Philippians 2:13 ICB) *Yes, God is working in you to help you want to do what pleases him. Then he gives you the power to do it.*
- **Day 2** (Philippians 3:14 TEV) *I run straight toward the goal in order to win the prize, which is God's call through Christ Jesus to the life above.*
- **Day 3** (James 1:2-4 ICB) *You will have many kinds of troubles. But when these things happen, you should be very happy. You know that these things are testing your faith. And this will give you patience. Let your patience show itself perfectly in what you do. Then you will be perfect and complete.*
- **Day 4** (1 Corinthians 10:13 ICB) *All the temptations that you have are the temptations that all people have. But you can trust God. He will not let you be tempted more than you can stand. But when you are tempted, God will also give you a way to escape that temptation. Then you will be able to stand.*
- **Day 5** (Romans 8:28-29 ICB) *We know that in everything God works for the good of those who love him. They are the people God called, because that was his plan. God knew them before he made the world. And God chose them to be like his Son.*
- **Day 6** (Romans 12:4-6 ICB) *The body has many parts. These parts all have different uses. In the same way, we are many, but in Christ we are all one body. And each part belongs to all the other parts. We*

83

all have different gifts. Each gift came because of the grace that God gave us.

- **Day 7** (Hebrews 10:24-25 TEV) *Let us be concerned for one another, to help one another to show love and to do good. Let us not give up the habit of meeting together, as some are doing. Instead, let us encourage one another all the more.*

The Sword of the Spirit

The Sword of the Spirit is an international, ecumenical association of Christian communities. You can learn more about the Sword of the Spirit by visiting its web site: www.swordofthespirit.net. Learn about the Sword of the Spirit in North America by visiting SOS-NAR.com.

Tabor House

Tabor House is the book publisher of the Sword of the Spirit. You can purchase books for and about Christian community at taborpub.com.

Made in the USA
Coppell, TX
03 March 2023